♦ All Glory, Laud, and Honor ♦

An Organ Suite for Holy Week

♦ Table of Contents ♦

www.FredBock.com

for Clinton and Barbara Flowers

All Glory, Laud, and Honor

Sw. Bourdon 8', Principal 4' Piccolo 2', Mixture IV
Gt. Diapason 8', Harmonic Flute 8', Octave 4', Twelfth 2-⅔', Mix. IV, Sw. to Gt. 8', Gt. to Gt. 8'
Ch. Festival Trumpet 8'
Ped. Diapason 16', Bourdon 16', Octave 8', Choralbass 4', Mixture IV, Trompette 8', Gt. to Ped.

MELCHIOR TESCHNER
Arranged by
CAROLYN HAMLIN (ASCAP)

In a festive style ♩ = 98

11
(Gt.)
15
20
Gt.
24
Ch.
(Gt.)

28
Gt.
Sw. Bourdon 8', Flute 4', Tierce 1⅗'
Ped. Violone 16', Gedeckt 8'
32
Sw.
36
40

Sw. Bourdon 8', Viola 8', Principal 4', Piccolo 2', Mix. IV
Gt. Diapason 8', Harmonic Flute 8', Octave 4', Twelfth 2⅔', Mix. IV., Sw. to Gt, 8', Ch. to Gt 8'
Ch. Gedeckt 8', Principal 4', Octave 1', Scharf III
Ped. Diapason 16', Bourdon 16', Octave 8', Mix. IV, Gt. to Ped, 8', Sw. to Ped. 8'

Sw. + Trumpet 8', Clarion 8'
Gt. + Tromba 8'
Ped. + Waldhorn 16'

Sw. Bourdon 8', Viola 8', Principal 4', Mix. IV, Waldhorn 16', Trumpet 8', Clarion 4'
Gt. Violone 16', Diapason 8', Harmonic Flute 8', Octave 4', Twelfth 2⅔', Fifteenth 2', Double Trumpet 16', Tromba 8', Mix. IV, Sw. to Gt. 8', Ch. to Gt. 8'
Ch. Gedeckt 8', Principal 4', Octave 4', Quintflute 1⅔', Scharf III
Ped. Diapason 16', Violone 16', Octave 8', Choralbass 4', Mix. IV, Trompette 8', Clarion 4', Gt. to Ped. 8', Sw. to Ped. 8', Ch. to Ped. 8'

Ped. +Bombarde 16'

Full Organ with Reeds
Slowing to end
rit.

for Rudy Lucente

Beneath the Cross of Jesus

Sw. Trumpet 8'
Gt. Diapason 8', Harmonic Flute 8', Flute 4', Ch. to Gt. 8'
Ch. Gedeckt 8', Principal 4'
Ped. Bourdon 16', Gt. to Ped. 8'

ST. CHRISTOPHER
Frederick C. Maker
Arr. by Carolyn Hamlin (ASCAP)

Passionately ♩ = 80

Sw. Viola 8', Viola Celeste 8', Bourdon 8', Flute Celeste II 8', Flute 4', Trem., Sw. to Gt. 8', Sw to Gt. 4', Ch. to Gt. 8'
Gt. Diapason 8', Gamba 8', Flute 4', Trem., Sw. to Gt. 8', Sw. to Gt. 4', Ch. to Gt. 8'
Ch. Viole 8', Viole Celeste 8', Gedeckt 8', Koppelflute 4', Trem., Sw. to Ch. 8',
Ped. Bourdon 32', Diapason 16', Bourdon 16', Octave 8', Gt. to Ped. 8', Sw. to Ped. 8'

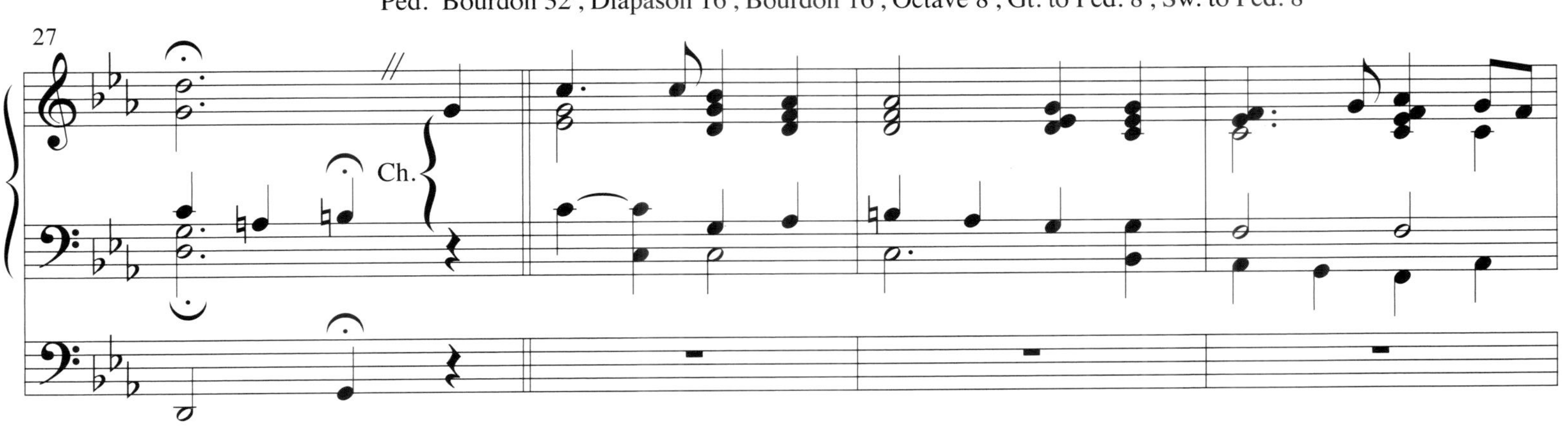

31
35
Gt.
39
43

Sw. Viola 8', Principal 4', Mix. IV, Trumpet 8'
Gt. Diapason 8', Octave 4', Twelfth 2⅔', Fifteenth 2', Tromba 8', Sw. to Gt. 8', Sw. to Gt. 4', Ch. to Gt. 8'
Ch. Gedeckt 8', Principal 4', Octave 2', Quintflute 1⅓'
Ped. Diapason 16', Bourdon 16', Violone 16', Octave 8', Choral Bass 4', Sw. to Ped. 8', Ch. to Ped. 8'

To previous registration, add:
Sw. Waldhorn 16' (or Bassoon), Clarion 4'
Gt. Violone 16', Double Trumpet 16'
Ch. Scharf III
Ped. Bourdon 32', Contre Bombarde 32', Bombarde 16'

for Martha Alter

Alas! and Did My Savior Bleed

with O Sacred Head, Now Wounded

Sw. Solo Reed 16' or 8'
Gt. Diapason 8', Flute 8'
Ch. Viole 8', Viole Celeste 8'
Ped. Bourdon 16', Ch. to Ped.

HUGH WILSON
Arranged by CAROLYN HAMLIN (ASCAP)

With passion ♩ = 82

15
20
Gt.
25
Gt. Add Octave 4'
Ped. Add Violone 16'
Gt.
30

O Sacred Head, Now Wounded
(Hans Leo Hassler)

Gt. Add Principal 2'

Gt. Add Flute 4'
Ped. Add Gt. to Ped.
55
Gt.
61
Sw. Flutes 8', 4', 2', Principal 4', Mixture
Gt. Principals 8', 4', 2', IV Mixture, Sw. to Gt.
Ch. Gedeckt 8', Principal 4', Octave 2', III Mix.
Ped. Diapason 16', Bourdon 16', Oct. 8', Gt. to Ped.
66
Gt.
70

74
79
rit.
Sw. Flute 8', Nazard 2⅔, Trem.
Gt. Flute Celeste 8'
Ped. Lieblich Gedeckt 16'
83
Gt.
Sw.
87
rit.

For Jeff Kirk

Crown Him with Many Crowns

GEORGE J. ELVEY
Arr. by Carolyn Hamlin (ASCAP)

Sw. Trumpet 8'
Gt. Principal 8', Harmonic Flute 8', Octave 4', Spitzflute 4', Ch. to Gt. 8'
Ch. Gedeckt 8', Principal 4', Koppelflute 4'
Ped. Bourdon 16', Violone 16', Gt. to Ped. 8', Ch. to Ped. 8'

With grandeur ♩ = 92

13
Gt.
17
(♭)
(♭)
21
3
slight rit.
Sw.
25
Sw.
a tempo
Ch.

8va
Gt.
slight rit.

Sw. Viola 8', Bourdon 8', Principal 4'
Gt. Diapason 8'; Flute 8', 4; Octave 4'; Fifteenth 2'; Sw. to Gt. 8; Ch. to Gt. 8'
Ch. Gedeckt 8', Principal 4', Koppelflute 4', Octave 2', Sw. to Ch. 8'
Ped. Bourdon 16', Violone 16', Octave 8', Sw. to Ped. 8'

Sw. Trumpet 8', Waldhorn 16', Clarion 4'
Gt. Principal 8', Harmonic Flute 8', Octave 4', Fifteenth 2', Mix. IV, Ch. to Gt. 8'
Ch. Gedeckt 8', Principal 4', Quintflute 1⅓', Flute 2'
Ped. Bourdon 16', Violone 16', Octave 8', Flute 8', Gt. to Ped. 8'

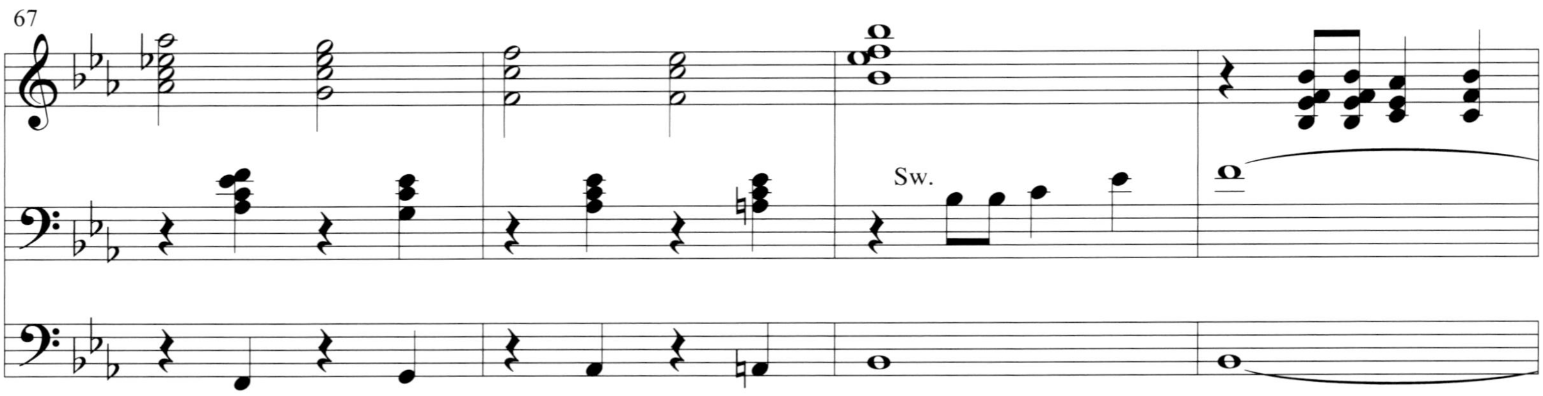

Sw. Viola 8', Bourdon 8' Principal 4', Trumpet 8', Waldhorn 16', Clarion 4', Mix. IV
Gt. Diapason 8', Harmonic Flute 8', Octave 4', Fifteenth 2', Mix. IV, Sw. to Gt. 8'
Ch. Festival Trumpet 8'
Ped. Diapason 16', Bourdon 16', Violone 16', Octave 8', Bombarde 16', Gt. to Ped. 8', Sw. to Ped. 8'

Maestoso

75
79
84
89
Full Organ with Reeds
Gt.